Succeeding with Money

A Financial Plan for Life

C. Pete Benson and Jon Maxson

CONTENTS

NOTES TO READERS

This publication contains the opinions and ideas of the authors. The strategies outlined in this book may not be suitable for every individual and are not guaranteed or warranted to produce any particular results. Presentation of performance data herein does not imply that similar results will be achieved in the future. Any such data are provided merely for illustrative and discussion purposes; rather than focusing on the time periods used or the results derived. The reader should focus instead on the underlying principles.

No warranty is made with respect to the accuracy or the completeness of the information contained herein, and both the authors and publisher specifically disclaim any responsibility for any liability, loss, or risk, personal or otherwise, that is incurred as a consequence, directly or indirectly, of the use and application of any of the contents of this book.

Lastly, this book is written under the right of the First Amendment to the Constitution of the United States. This book is written as an outside business activity from our investment advisory business.

The ideas expressed are not meant to be taken as advice that you can just go act upon in every case. You should find an individual advisor that you can trust to implement these ideas after determining if they are appropriate and suitable for your unique situation.

INTRODUCTION

This book is all about *Succeeding With Money* and ways to make that happen. Who doesn't want that? All of us are either retired or on the road to building our future retirement, and we need all the help we can get.

This writing is more like a booklet than a book. The purpose is to present basic concepts to help motivate the reader to 'get started' thinking about and acting on their family's financial plan to build a secure plan for their money. It is certainly not meant to be a be-all and end-all, but simply meant to help you get your plan jump started. Our goal has been to keep things simple and take away the mystique and intimidation many feel about financial matters and especially reading a book about it. The goal here is to be practical and pragmatic, not talk theory and economic policy. Some have said, 'knowledge is power'. We believe only "applied knowledge is powerful". Information is not enough, it's all about **implementation**! As you read each of these chapters, we recommend you put the book down and write down 3 things you need to implement about each topic, then write down a due date to have that thing accomplished, and lastly talk to someone you trust to help keep you accountable this year in your financial goals. Then, and only then, do we feel that real life change will happen.

CHAPTER 1:
IN RETIREMENT IT'S ALL ABOUT INCOME!

A key aspect to maximizing retirement money is investing with a bias towards income-producing securities and products. In your retirement years, income is the outcome!

KNOW WHICH ANNUITIES TO STEER CLEAR OF AND THE ONES TO STRONGLY CONSIDER

What are income- producing securities and products? These are investments designed to produce income but could also provide some growth in the particular investment. Let's talk about the real basic difference between a growth type investment and an income type investment. A growth type investment is typically one that you're going to buy, like shares in the technology company Linked-ln. It's an investment that does not pay an income so you don't get a dividend from it. You just buy the shares, hope the shares are going to go up in value, and don't want any current income while you hold the shares. That's an example of a growth investment.

An example of a growth and income (or income-producing investment) could be if you own, for instance, stock in a company that pays a big dividend. A company like AT&T pays a very nice dividend and usually the dividend on AT&T is somewhere around 4-5%. So you can buy the shares and hope the shares go up, but while you are holding the shares you're continuing to get dividends (income) on the shares. So you're getting paid to hold the stock, if you will. That's an example of a growth and income investment.

What we want to do if we're interested in maximizing retirement income is to have a goal towards more income or have a bias towards more income-producing assets.

Now these could be annuities. It could be real estate investment trusts which are referred to as REITs. These could be high yielding bonds, stocks that pay dividends, or oil and gas master-limited partnerships that pay very high dividends. We're going to go through some of these different things. Please understand that we're not recommending one of these or all of these to you in your individual situation. It is critical that you get with somebody who is a knowledgeable financial advisor who you can trust and can help show you the pros and the cons, the good and the bad, about these different investments so that you can sift through and filter out the things that are not right for you.

ANNUITIES

The last tool we will discuss with a bias towards an income-producing account is an annuity, and there are four different types of annuities. We are going to go through these very, very briefly then we're going to hone in on one particular annuity which is an annuity designed for income where you don't have to give up control of your principal.

Annuity number one is just simply a **fixed annuity**. If you understand the CD (certificate of deposit), you understand the fixed annuity. You can go out and buy a five-year fixed annuity which means you deposit your money with an insurance company and you leave it alone for five years. Right now you may earn a 3% interest rate each year for the five years, and then at the end of that five years you can take your money and you do whatever you want with it. So you made a time commitment for five years. And you get 3% for five years.

That's a lot like a five-year CD. It's not issued by a bank, and it's not FDIC insured, but that is a fixed annuity. It's quite simple actually. You get principal protection, a set interest rate, some liquidity (often 10% annually) and also tax deferral if you choose to leave the interest in the account all five years.

The second type of annuity is a **variable annuity**. In a variable annuity you're still buying an account from an insurance company but inside that annuity are all kinds of mutual fund choices called sub-accounts. You still have stock market risks in a variable annuity on the principal. However, in a variable annuity for an extra fee inside the account you can get a minimum income guarantee.

Right now there's a company out there, where as a 65-year-old you could put $500,000 into the variable annuity and they will guarantee you 5% income from that for as long as you live. You also get to pick those sub-accounts or the investments inside that annuity.

Also, if your picks are really bad and the account goes to zero, as long as you don't take out more than the 5% per year, the insurance company is still going to pay you the 5% for as long as you live. That's called a variable annuity with an income rider or an income guarantee on it. That can be pretty attractive if you want the upside of the market. Again, the variable annuity gives you some upside potential of the market, but you also carry the downside risk of the market. However, you do have a minimum guarantee on your income if you choose to structure it that way.

The third type of annuity is an **immediate annuity**, and that just simply means you take your money and you give it to the insurance company. So you've given up control of your money. If you give the same $500,000 to the insurance company as a 65-year-old they might guarantee you 6.5% payout on that money for as long as you live.

Here though, you've given up access to your principal, and you actually don't own the $500,000 anymore. They're giving you the 6.5% payout for as long as you live but you could die before you get all of the $500,000 out. The insurance company then usually keeps all the leftover funds in most cases. However, if you live really long, then you could possibly beat the insurance company at their own game.

These first three annuities aren't as popular with our firm as the next one we are going to tell you about which we use a lot for income planning purposes in our financial services practice for our clients. This is called an index annuity, and in particular the **index annuity** with a guaranteed minimum income rider on it. Let's talk about this. With the index annuity, you can take that $500,000 and put it in an account. Your principal is guaranteed by the insurance company. If the stock market index drops, you lose no money. If the index goes up, you can earn interest based on that index. Now you're not going to get as much interest as you would have in the good years if your money was directly invested in the stock market. Your upside is subject to a cap. You are giving up some upside potential in return for the insurance company taking away the downside risk.

Now again, there are a lot more details than this but we're trying to keep the conversation simple here. The bottom line is that you have principal protection and over time you can get a reasonable rate of return on the index annuity that should be higher than a CD or a fixed annuity if we look back over history. You can add to the index annuity what we call an income rider, which can be very powerful. There's one company out there right now where you can put in let's say that $500,000 and they'll guarantee you a 7% increase in your income account value for every year that you leave the account alone. If you leave it for ten years, the <u>income</u> value on that $500,000 would become around $1 million. Now you can't just take out that $1 million in one lump sum but what you can do is can take income off of that, a percentage of income off of that $1 million account value. That $1 million could pay you out as much as 5%, 5.5%, or even 6% depending on your age. So you've invested an original amount of maybe $500,000. You've waited for ten years. And then maybe you can get $60,000 a year guaranteed for as long as you live, and it perhaps may pay out even more than your original premium.

Now with these annuities, there are a lot of details we are not going into here. So please understand, we're not recommending an annuity for everyone. This becomes a one-on-one conversation that needs to happen with a good financial advisor for you, but it's certainly worth investigating. (By the way we have never heard of anyone at a big stock brokerage firm recommend these products. We will let you figure out why).

DIVIDEND-PAYING STOCKS

Stocks that pay dividends are traditionally more mature companies. Let us just rattle off some names here. These are all stocks that currently pay nice dividends. Some of them we own, some we do not own: Chevron, Exxon, IBM, Apple Computer, Pfizer, Merck, AT&T, Ford, and Verizon. These are all companies where if you own their stock, yes, you're hoping the shares go up over time but you're getting paid to hold the stock. Let's take Chevron stock for instance. Say you owned Chevron stock for a number of years, and when you bought it, it was paying about a 3% dividend. If you put $100,000 into it for example, you're getting paid $3,000 per year to own the stock.

Now let's think about the safety of that investment for a minute. If you are getting paid $3,000 a year to own the stock and you put in $100,000, that's obviously a 3% yield. If you put that $100,000 in the bank at the same time you had bought the Chevron stock, you likely would not be receiving a 3% yield. Currently you would probably only be getting 1% yield. Also, if you put that money in the bank you wouldn't get any growth on my money. All you are guaranteed is to get your money back. With Chevron stock, you don't have a guarantee, but in our opinion Chevron is not likely going to go out of business. Therefore, we think that not only is your investment somewhat secure, even though you know the price of the shares will fluctuate, you're getting paid 3% dividend and over time Chevron has increased its dividends. So your yield on the original investment may also be going up. That's an example of a high dividend paying stock.

Now you have to understand that in the income- producing investment category, dividend-paying stocks certainly do carry stock market risk and fluctuation because they are going to go up and down in value year after year. It's an important part of the whole picture here when you're considering income-producing securities.

EQUITY INCOME TYPE MUTUAL FUNDS AND ETF'S

The second category would be equity income type mutual funds and ETF's (Exchange Traded Funds). So if you don't want to get into picking stocks you can pick mutual funds or ETF's. In a mutual fund, the mutual fund itself owns a group or a bundle of stocks. Let's take a fund called Fidelity Equity Income Fund. Well, Fidelity Equity Income Fund might own 100 or 200 different stocks or different companies within that fund. You buy one fund but there's a money manager at Fidelity that goes through and chooses the stocks that he thinks are the best ones to own.

Now all those stocks or most of those stocks are going to pay a dividend. So you could have them pay you out the dividends that the stocks inside that fund are paying and that dividend yield is sometimes 2-3%. In addition to the dividend, the share price of the mutual fund may go up if they're picking good companies inside the mutual fund because of course those company shares underlying the mutual fund also hope to go up in value. So again, you're getting growth and income from this investment. It works very similar with Exchange Traded Funds.

Many of these ETF's we look for have very low fees and can pay generous dividends and income.

As you realized from these first two categories, dividend-paying stocks and equity income type mutual funds – you may only get somewhere around a 2-3% yield unless you buy super high yielding dividend-paying stocks. Let's just say you buy the normal ones that are going to pay you about a 3% dividend. That may not be enough income for you but you're also hoping to get price appreciation. So maybe you don't have your whole portfolio in equity income funds or dividend-paying stocks but you have a portion of it invested this way. Because the equity income mutual fund and the dividend-paying stocks over time should appreciate in value, you also have some inflation protection.

HIGH YIELD BONDS

When appropriate, we like to consider high yield bonds for a portion of someone's portfolio when income is desired. An example of a high yield bond could be a bond by a company like Verizon, which most of us are familiar with. While they're not as safe necessarily as General Electric or Wal-Mart, they still seem to be a solid company and you might be able to buy a Verizon bond that pays a 5-6% interest rate. That would be a very nice interest rate. You'll notice the interest rate is higher than the dividend-paying stocks and that's mostly because it's a bond. From a legal standpoint, a bond from a company is normally safer than a stock from the same company.

You can consider bond funds, high yield bond funds, and high yield exchange traded funds in your portfolio. You possibly could build out a portfolio to give you 4.5-5.5% income yield. It may pay a very nice income that you can spend right now if you want to, and although the share price will go up and down, it may be fairly stable over time. Historically speaking, if you look back at the writing of this book over the last ten years, a good basket of high yield bond funds or a mutual fund or an exchange traded fund, the historical total rate of return on that is somewhere around 6-7% without as much volatility as the stock market. At this time though interest rates are still very low, and they have begun to rise slightly so do a complete and full investigation before you decide whether this may be right for you or be sure to find a competent financial advisor to assist you.

REAL ESTATE TRUSTS AND INTERVAL FUNDS

Over time real estate has been one of the best performing assets to own when it comes to inflation and in addition to that, commercial real estate, whether it's apartment buildings, office buildings, warehouses or retail facilities like Wal-Mart, CVS, or Home Depot - they often spin off rental income.

There are two types of real estate trusts. There is a non-traded real estate trust and also a publicly traded real estate trust. A traded real estate trust trades just like a stock. They tend to pay lower dividends and the share price bounces up and down every single day in the stock market. A non-traded real estate trust does not trade like a stock. In fact, you give up liquidity when you buy a non-traded real estate trust. For example, you may personally own a non-traded real estate trust and let's say it's healthcare properties all around the U.S. You could possibly enjoy a 5.5-6.5% dividend from that and most of them pay monthly. So if you put $50,000 into it, you should receive that dividend every month that you can take for income or you could just have it stay in the account and compound. Please understand that dividends in any investment can go up or down and completely away in certain cases.

Over time you are expecting the value of the real estate to go up, so it also may act as an inflation hedge. This can be very attractive for someone who is getting ready to retire or is in retirement. Because remember, the key in retirement is when you're taking income off a portfolio, you want to try to limit the stock market risk. So if the market goes way down and you continue to pull income off a portfolio it's going to either erode the portfolio down to zero over time, or you're going to have to cut your income back because now you have to sell more shares to produce that income. You're in a much better position with something where the share price is more stable and you can spend the dividends and hopefully get appreciation on the share price. That way you are less likely to have to sell when the market is low. So we consider this non-traded real estate trust when suitable for our clients - and again folks, don't go out and buy these on your own.

One of the more popular ways we now include real estate is to utilize "Interval Funds". Give us a call and speak to a professional advisor who knows these investments.

All of these things that we've mentioned, the dividend-paying stocks, the equity income type mutual funds, the high yield bonds and high yield bond funds, the real estate funds, and the annuities may produce a nice income for you that may be much higher than some of the things you're using now and many are somewhat removed from stock market volatility, depending on which category that you tend to use.

In this chapter we have talked about investing with a bias towards income-producing securities and products. The reason this is so important is because so many families that we meet with that come in for an appointment at our firm have been trying to do everything with just mutual funds. They've been trying to create a secure retirement with mutual funds. They have a basket of mutual funds whether it's in their 401(k) or elsewhere and they're moving towards retirement within five years or maybe they're in retirement already and they're just riding this roller coaster of the stock market. Up one year, down the next, up for a few years and then the big down. It's causing all kinds of problems in their lives emotionally and quite frankly, they're losing sleep at night. Consequently, they are looking for a better way to provide income.

Our answer to that is to have a bias towards income-producing investments. As a retiree, let's say you're sixty-five-years old. Maybe you ought to have 65-75% of your money in income-producing assets and maybe 25-35% of your money is actually in pure stock or growth mutual funds. If you have adequate income from Social Security and pensions, perhaps you don't need that much, but many families do. Again, it's not a one size fits all, so please meet personally with your trusted advisor or coach.

CHAPTER 2:
CUSTOM DESIGN YOUR FINANCIAL PLAN

How unfortunate it is that people will spend as many as 80,000 hours working for more than 40 years and yet not spend the time necessary to map out their finances and plan for their retirement. From our vantage point as financial advisors, far too many people seem to be ambling aimlessly along, hoping and praying that everything will just turn out all right. Hope is not a plan!

All through our lives we need to be following a plan of some kind. In our earlier years, we need to follow a budget. We must set aside an emergency fund, plan for children's education, plan how and when we are going to buy our next car, decide when and whether we are going to purchase or rent a home.

Before the days of the GPS (Global Positioning System) we had the good, old-fashioned road map. It was unthinkable for a family to go off on a long vacation involving automobile travel to unfamiliar places without first obtaining a road map on which to mark out the route. As a matter of fact, at every gas station there was a rack of complimentary road maps. They were free with a fill-up. Sadly, the vast majority of Americans spend more time planning their next vacation than they do planning the rest of their lives in retirement.

(The following story told by Pete Benson illustrates the importance of planning)

A few years ago my wife Ginnie and I were invited to hold a financial conference in Velden, Austria, for a group of missionaries who had come together from their assignments all over Europe. It was a long trip from central Tennessee to Austria and back, so Ginnie and I decided to make a two-week vacation out of it.

For several months, in our spare time, we got on the internet to search out various places we wanted to visit on the trip. It was daunting, trying to figure out which cities and countries we wanted to visit. We also tried to iron out which hotels we would stay in but there were thousands to pick from.

Then there were the little niggling details about transportation; what was the best way to get from place to place? We had no idea. There was conflicting advice on the internet and it was difficult to find unbiased information. The big pieces of the puzzle were clear to us; we wanted to spend a day or two in Paris, visit Germany, and see Venice and Rome. What we couldn't put together were the details of how to do that in the most efficient manner.

> **YOU NEED A STRATEGIC AND CUSTOM DESIGNED PLAN**

We worked on it a few months ourselves, but as the time for the trip approached we were feeling less and less confident. We decided to swallow our pride and hire a professional to map it all out for us. We had no idea what a pleasant experience this would be.

When the travel agent met with us, we knew we had made the right decision. She asked us dozens of questions to get a feel for what we really wanted out of the trip and then mapped out a wonderful tour for us. She left nothing to chance; all the details were neatly buttoned up. On the last visit to the travel agent's office she presented us with a thick book consisting of every detail of the trip from beginning to end. We knew the times of every flight, how to get to every hotel, train station, restaurant and village along the way.

Our delightful, 13-day European vacation took us through four countries without a single hitch. We were so thankful that we didn't try "winging it" the way we started. Who knows where we would have ended up had it not been for the assistance of a fully-trained, competent, professional travel planner?

Who knows if it really happened or not, but the story is told that Albert Einstein, the famous physicist, was once traveling on a train when the conductor came down the aisle, punching the tickets of every passenger. When he came to Einstein, the bushy-haired scientist fumbled around in his vest pockets. He couldn't find his ticket, so he searched his trouser pockets. It wasn't there, so he looked in his briefcase but couldn't find it. Then he looked in the seat beside him. He still couldn't find it.

The conductor said, "Dr. Einstein, I know who you are. We all know who you are. I'm sure you bought a ticket. Don't worry about it."

Einstein nodded appreciatively. The conductor continued down the aisle punching tickets. As he was ready to move to the next car, he turned around and saw the famous man down on his hands and knees looking under his seat for his ticket.

The conductor rushed back and said, "Dr. Einstein, Dr. Einstein, don't worry, I know who you are. No problem. You don't need a ticket. I'm sure you bought one."

Einstein looked at him and said, "Young man, I too, know who I am. But without my ticket I have no idea where I'm going."

The point of the story is that traveling without a destination is pointless.

Several quotes exist in the archives of literature about this. Author Lewis Carroll (*Alice in Wonderland*) is quoted as saying: "If you don't know where you are going, any road will get you there." Actually, the quote is a paraphrased rendering of a conversation between Alice and the Cheshire Cat in chapter six of Carroll's famous book. "Would you tell me, please, which way I ought to go from here?"

"That depends a good deal on where you want to get to," said the Cat.

"I don't much care where--" said Alice.

"Then it doesn't matter which way you go," said the Cat.

The most colorful quote, however, is attributed to Yogi Berra, the master of the unintentional (maybe) malapropism. There are actually two versions of this quote:

"If you don't know where you are going, you might wind up someplace else," and "You've got to be very careful if you don't know where you are going, because you might not get there." Whether the famous Yankee catcher ever actually uttered either one or not, it still makes the point splendidly that to get anywhere you must have a destination in mind.

As financial advisors, such a concept is a core belief for us. *You never plan to fail…you just fail to plan.* We are big believers that successful people – in every area of life, but especially financially – are planners.

It's even Biblical to plan.

Proverbs 22:3 - "A prudent man foresees the difficulties ahead and prepares (PLANS) for them; the simpleton goes blindly on and suffers the consequences."

Luke 14:28 - "But don't begin until you count the cost. For who would begin construction of a building without first calculating the cost to see if there is enough money to finish it?" – The Living Bible.

DETERMINE VALUES AND SET GOALS

Planning starts with making some simple (often not easy, but simple) decisions and putting them down in writing.

Values - What are the most important things in life to you? Have you ever listed them? This is a crucial step in planning. It's like plotting your destination before a trip. These values may change over time. For example, when you are young and just starting out in life, your values may center on entertainment, nice cars and a big home. Later it may be providing an education for your children or becoming debt-free. Still later on in life, your values may lean more in the direction of providing an income for retirement, traveling, giving money to your church or other charities, or perhaps arranging your affairs so that you are able to retire early. Whatever the case, name your top five values in order of priority and write them down. Why is it important to put them in writing? One reason is that this very exercise forces you to organize them. Also, putting your values in writing sets you up nicely for the second step.

Goals - Set your goals. If values are the destination, then goals represent the road-map which will take you there.

Charles Schulz, creator of the cartoon strip Peanuts, was capable of conveying many thought-provoking ideas through the little round-headed children he drew. We heard about one where the strip's protagonist, Charlie Brown, appears in the first frame pulling back the string of a bow. The arrow is pointed slightly up. We can't see the target but we assume he is shooting at something.

In the second frame we see Charlie Brown over by a fence where his

31

arrow has embedded itself in the wood.

In the third frame, Charlie Brown is painting a bullseye around the arrow.

Then Lucy comes running up in the last frame and says, "Charlie Brown, you blockhead! That's not how you do it!" To which Charlie Brown responds: "But this way, Lucy, I never miss."

Do you know anyone who operates that way regarding their finances? Hoping for success with no goal in mind? Charlie Brown made no apologies for taking such a shortcut, did he? In fact, he rationalized that if he had no target he couldn't miss! When it comes to financial matters that is unfortunately how many people go through life.

THE "TYRANNY OF THE URGENT"

In the 1960s, Charles Hummel published a little booklet called "Tyranny of the Urgent", which quickly became a best seller and a business classic. In it, Hummel pointed out that there is a regular tension between things that are urgent and things that are important. Far too often, says Hummel, the urgent wins.

In the business world the urgent demands of your boss, your client, or petty office relationships, can often take priority over important things like thoroughly completing a task before starting the next one, or building unity in a work team which would instill camaraderie and longevity. The urgent, though less important, gets priority, while the important is put on the back burner. That's why it is tyrannical. While you are yielding to that impulse, greasing the squeaky wheel, you are delayed from your destination.

In Charlie Brown's case, he didn't aim and then shoot; he shot and then aimed. How convenient it is to just draw a target where your arrow lands! Charlie Brown, like many people, wanted instant gratification with no effort. What is our "tyranny of the urgent"? And how do we know we are hitting the target (goal) if there is no target (we have not set a goal)?

When it comes to financial planning, it always helps to have an "accountability partner" to help you keep on track with accomplishing your goals. You cannot work your plan if you don't have one. Once you have one, it won't succeed unless you work it. Put succinctly, "plan your work… and work your plan."

So, then that leads us to the BIG question for you, "Do you have a written, well thought out financial plan? You know, a short term plan for saving and spending your money, also a mid-term plan, and how about a long term plan?" Most people's plan is "I think so, I hope so, maybe". You mean that's it? At our firm, we are planners. You need a strategic and custom designed plan! Every family needs this. At Beacon Capital Management, we will work with you to design and implement this plan!!!

CHAPTER 3:
SECRETS TO REDUCING FEES AND TAXES

It's not how much you make on your money it's how much you get to KEEP!!! Fees and taxes can be the enemy to your overall return. The sexy and exciting part of investing is chasing performance, but those who have been successful in investing overall know that reducing fees and taxes is paramount.

FEES

There are many different kinds of fees associated with your funds and overall portfolio. There are sales loads, deferred sales loads, turnover and transaction fees, fund management fees, advisor fees, 12B-1 fees, soft dollar costs, P/E ratios, brokerage fees, custodial fees, and more to be aware of. Some funds have less than 1% in fees and many funds have fees ranging between 1-2.5% annually.

There are times you get what you pay for, and there are times you do not get what you pay for. Bottom line---fees matter! So how does an investor find out exactly what they may be paying in fees overall. Well, we would suggest that one of the most important things you can do is to go and get a second opinion from an advisor who will do a very detailed analysis of all your fees for you. It will save you a lot of time because researching and finding all those hidden fees can be a very tedious process. You may need to read a lot of pages of various prospectuses and then you would need to be able to interpret and add up all the fees. It's an almost impossible task.

At Beacon Capital Management we pay for software that can drill down and give specifically all the fees in any account or fund you may have whether it's a mutual fund, a bond fund, an ETF, a managed account, a variable annuity, e t c. If you don't know your fees, how do you know if you are paying too much, or if you are getting a good deal? Also, as important as fees are, they are not the only consideration.

What is really vital is this, "Are you getting value from the fees you are paying?"

TAXES

At the time of this writing, the historic Tax Reform Bill has just passed and been signed by President Donald Trump. There may never have been a more important time to make sure you are working with a financial firm that focuses on taxes and possible tax saving strategies.

IT'S NOT JUST HOW MUCH YOU MAKE ON YOUR MONEY, IT'S HOW MUCH YOU GET TO KEEP

At Beacon, tax saving ideas and methods are high on our priority list for our clients.

There are all kinds of taxes, but one of the clear keys to having more money available to spend is to pay less in taxes. Now we're certainly not talking about cheating on your taxes; that is not the intent of this chapter. The objective is to make sure that you are smart about where your investments are; where you're taking your income from, so that you don't pay more taxes than you absolutely have to. We want you to pay the minimum amount of taxes because that just simply means more money in your pocket.

We've had clients come into our firm and after doing a study of their tax return and where their investments are; sometimes we're able to save them a significant amount of taxes, not only by reducing their income tax but also by reducing taxes on their Social Security.

One of the things we want you to understand is how the different types of income (earned, social security, interest) get taxed. So let's talk about some of these types of taxes here.

There are about five different types of taxes we're going to discuss. Number one is traditional income tax. Number two is taxes on your Social Security income. The third type is capital gains tax. The fourth category is taxes you pay when you take money out of your IRA or 401(k) or any other type of retirement account. The fifth type we want to talk about is taxes on annuities. So let's dig in.

Income taxes - Let's discuss traditional income taxes. Taxes we pay on our earned income or on our pension income and also on any kind of deferred compensation payout we're getting from a former employer. If we're exercising stock options, all that falls into the area of income taxes. You need to be aware of where and when you can reduce your income taxes. Again, really what this comes down to is do you need all of the income that you're paying income taxes on? Sometimes there are ways to defer income. So we're not going to spend a lot of time here on income taxes, but just think of traditional income taxes differently than Social Security taxes which we will talk about next.

Income taxes are any taxes on all of your income: earned income, unearned income, rental income, interest, dividends, distribution from retirement plans, etc. This might get confusing and you might say here, "well Pete and Jon, you just talked about how interest and dividends affect my Social Security taxes". Yes, we did. But that was your Social Security income that's being taxed. Now we're talking about potential double taxation, if you will, because it's on your other income. Any time you can reduce income while still having spendable money in retirement, you may be hitting a home run there. But again, that depends on your individual situation. So just be aware of your income taxes.

One trick that many clients have employed is that they'll take a certain amount of income in one year. Maybe they take $60,000 in one year and then they can manipulate their income so they take much lower income in the second year. So then maybe they're living off of let's say $40,000 a year, but taking $60,000 one year and then only $20,000 the next. Well, the year that they're only taking $20,000 what's happening is they might not owe any income taxes at all. They might not pay any taxes on their Social Security either. So it's a way of staggering income tax. For more details on that or how we've been able to successfully employ that with clients, feel free to call our office.

Social Security Income - Now, let's talk about Social Security taxes. Many of you were told that when you become retired and get monthly Social Security checks you won't have to pay taxes on that money. As a matter of fact, that was the intent of Social Security; that the payments you received in retirement would be tax-free. Well, that's not the case for a number of different reasons. The politicians have gone after Social Security and most of you have to include it in your taxable income when you retire. So if you're already retired you've learned this lesson. If you're not retired, you need to understand this.

People don't always pay taxes on their Social Security income. Sometimes 50% of this income is exposed to taxes, meaning that if you get $20,000 a year in Social Security you have to pay taxes on $10,000 of it. For some folks, 85% of their Social Security income is exposed to the taxman. Meaning again, for that $20,000 income from Social Security that you may be getting, $17,000 or 85% is exposed to taxes. What's the difference? The Social Security check can be the same. That $20,000 you're receiving from Social Security can be exactly the same as your next door neighbor is getting but depending on where your other income comes from, you could be exposed to higher taxes. So, let's talk about some things that could trigger taxes on your Social Security. The two big ones are interest and dividends. There's also a third one; which is tax-free income from municipal bonds.

Let's discuss interest that affects tax on Social Security for a minute. Many of the folks we meet have money at the bank, and that money is in CDs, and it's in CDs because they feel that is keeping their money safe. With CDs not being exposed to the stock market and being held at the bank it gives a sense of safety to these folks. Well, of course the CDs pay interest and most folks that have CDs at the bank don't take the interest. They leave the interest at the bank. They let the interest roll back or reinvest in the CD. However, at the end of the year, they would have to declare that as income on your tax return, and that additional interest income on your tax return goes into a formula that could trigger taxes on your Social Security.

Other types of interest income could be from mutual funds. If you have a bond fund, there is interest paid on those bonds. You, like most of our clients, are likely reinvesting that interest. When you have a mutual fund, the fund pays a distribution at the end of the year; you just buy more shares. You don't even know what's happening sometimes. Yet that shows up on your tax return potentially triggering a tax on your Social Security.

The other big item that impacts tax on Social Security is dividends. Now dividends are nice because they get taxed at a lower rate if they're qualified dividends. But dividends overall, whether they're qualified or not qualified, show up on your tax return. What happens is the IRS says okay, we're going to add up all your interest, all your dividends, all your tax-free municipal bond interest. After we add up all those numbers, we're going to take half of your Social Security and we're going to add all your other income, like pension income and earned income and so on. That is your "Provisional Income". We're going to add all that up and if you trigger a certain threshold, then you will be subject to Social Security taxes.

So the key here is not to pay taxes on interest and dividends that you're not using if possible. Let me give you an example. We talked earlier about money at the bank. The money that's in a CD is earning interest and you're not spending the interest; it's just rolling into the bank. You're reinvesting the interest into the CD. However, it's being added to your tax return. What if you had that same money in a fixed annuity? Fixed annuities are relatively safe. They're not FDIC insured, but the principal is protected from market risk. You can take out the interest being paid out on that fixed annuity, but if you're not receiving the interest, if you're just letting it roll into the annuity, you don't have to declare that as taxable income. Now, obviously, you have to make a time commitment with the annuity like you do with a CD, but if you can defer those taxes you're saving taxes on your Social Security income. Get more information before investing, but it certainly is one idea to consider.

Another idea is instead of mutual funds that pay big dividends at the end of the year, buy more tax efficient mutual funds, especially if you're not pulling the dividends out and spending them. You can own exchange traded funds or tax efficient mutual funds that don't spin out those distributions every year and then, of course, you won't have to add that to your taxable income. The key on Social Security taxes is really paying attention to the other things that are going on in your tax return. This is what we help families with all the time when they come in and visit with us at our firm. We often look at their tax return and make sure before we start analyzing their investments that they are not paying more taxes than is absolutely necessary.

Capital Gains Taxes - Another type of tax is capital gains. These taxes are when we sell something and have to pay a tax because we made a profit. Hopefully it's long-term capital gains. Short-term capital gains, when we sell something we've owned for less than a year, are taxed as ordinary income. So, if you buy a share of Exxon stock today and six months from now you sell it at a profit, that is a short- term capital gain and that's going to get taxed just like regular income, at a higher tax bracket. But if you have long-term gains, an asset owned for more than one year, long-term gains for most of us are taxed at a much lower tax bracket.

There are a few areas where long-term gains come into play for our clients. Number one could be a stock that was inherited. So let's say your mom or dad pass away and you inherited Apple stock, and let's pretend you inherited it ten years ago when it was worth a lot less money. Well when you inherit that stock, that's your ownership date for the purpose of establishing your tax cost. Now it's ten years later and you go to sell that Apple stock. Well, it's capital gains tax. It's a long-term capital gain. So you get to add that on a different part of your return, and you're only taxed at either 15% or 20% where on your regular income you could be taxed up to as much as 35-37%. So you can see how capital gains, long-term capital gains tax is much more favorable than ordinary income taxes. That's why it's very advantageous to own either individual stocks or exchange traded funds where there's not a lot of buying and selling going on in the exchange traded funds. Of course, with individual stocks, you get to control when the buying and selling is going on because then you don't have to pay taxes on money that you are not currently using. The compound effect of owning assets over a long period of time without having to pay taxes is absolutely phenomenal. We cannot express how exciting it is to own something like a piece of real estate or shares of stock, or maybe a piece of a business, that goes up in value, even if it's only increasing by 8-12% per year, just for the fact that you're not paying taxes on it. Then when you do sell it, you get to use the proceeds but you only have to pay the long-term capital gains tax rates on it which is very, very powerful. To wrap up the subject of capital gains taxes; short-term means you've owned the asset for less than a year and long-term simply means you've owned the asset for more than a year.

IRA, 401(K) & Other Retirement Plan Distributions - One of the other ways to reduce your taxes in retirement is to get control of your IRA and 401(k), and other retirement plan distributions. What do we mean by get control? We simply mean that at age 70 ½ the IRS forces us to begin taking distributions from any qualified retirement plans, which are IRAs, 401(k)s, 457 plans, 403(b) plans, and a few other less common plans.

The IRS forces us to take those distributions. There's only one exception to this, and that is if we have a 401(k) with a company that we're still working for. If we have a 401(k) with a company we're still working for then we don't have to take our required minimum distribution out of that particular 401(k).

Now this brings up an interesting possibility. What if you are working for a company, let's say Coca Cola? You're seventy-two years old. Still working there as an employee, and you have a 401(k) with them. You also have other IRAs and other retirement accounts and you'd just as soon not have to take money out of those other accounts because you don't need the income right now, but the IRS is forcing you to take money out of those other IRAs or retirement accounts because of course you're over 70 ½. You could actually take that money, roll it into the 401(k) at the company and now you don't have to take required minimum distributions on that Coca Cola 401(k) until again, you leave that company and job.

The next thing that happens is the IRS comes along and says we're also going to have you lose control on your retirement accounts. The key here is to get out in front of these required minimum distributions.

Quite frankly, start thinking about this when you're sixty and sixty-five years old and saying well, if the IRS is going to take control of these retirement accounts and force me to start taking money out at age 70 ½, maybe I should come up with a plan when I'm sixty or sixty-five, or even sixty-eight to begin to reduce the potential force out of those accounts at age 70 ½. There are a couple of things you can do here. One is you could at age sixty-five for instance, freeze the growth of your IRA. Say every time your IRA goes up in value, you're going to start taking a little bit of money. Let us give you an example here. Let's say you have $1 million in non-retirement accounts or we could say you have $1 million in brokerage accounts. This could be broken up into different types of annuities, maybe different types of financial products or funds. You have $1 million saved up and it's not in IRAs. You decide out of that $1 million you want about a $60,000 a year income and you want that to last for the rest of your life. Six percent income, then, is the goal.

Well, there are a number of ways you could do that. You could invest in different securities or different insurance products and just spin off $60,000 a year and spend it, but that would mean your income is $60,000 a year and you have to pay taxes on that entire $60,000 a year. That may not be favorable. Another thing you could do is come up with a little trick called a laddered annuity plan, or a structured income plan. There are different names that advisors call it. That would look something like this:

You take that $1 million and divide it up into four sections. The first section would be probably about $270,000. You take that $270,000 and buy a five-year immediate annuity (SPIA), which means that you're giving that $270,000 to an insurance company and they're going to guarantee to pay you out all that money over the next five years. You are going to get a little bit of interest, so you'll probably get about $60,000 a year for five years based on current rates.

Now what that means is when they pay you out that $60,000 for the first five years, remember $270,000 will be your original investment, and only $30,000 over that five- year period was interest. If you take the $30,000 of total interest you will get over five years, divide that by five, that's about $6,000 of interest per year. That means you are getting $60,000 of spendable money per year and you are only paying income tax on $6,000 of it. So for the first five years of the retirement income that's coming off of that $1 million portfolio it's almost all tax free. In fact, it may all be tax free if you don't have too much other income as we discussed earlier.

Now what happens is at the end of the five-year period you have spent down that $270,000, and you've got to tap into the next leg or the next rung of the annuity ladder that you've built. But the next rung of that annuity ladder is still going to be very tax-favored. Maybe for years six through ten, 70% of your income is completely tax free.

The idea you can see already is that you're spending down these different pieces of money. So you've taken the first bucket and spent it down to zero. You're now taking the second bucket from year's six to ten and spending it down to zero. The idea is buckets three and four are growing, and they should be growing faster than what you're spending down and therefore, you are keeping up. So if you pass away, your heirs potentially could get your original investment amount back, especially if you layer life insurance into it.

We're not trying to get into all the details of this laddered annuity strategy. We just want you to understand the power of that first five years, and maybe even the second five years, where much of your retirement income can be completely tax free. What that means is in the years when you are probably most active - traveling, visiting the kids and the grandkids, spending more money- you're potentially paying less in taxes. Now in the later years of your retirement, maybe in your late seventies and eighties, yes, you're going to have to pay taxes just as you would have if that would have all been ordinary income, all that $60,000, but maybe you don't care as much then. It's about getting more money in your pocket in the early years of your retirement.

These different ways to lower taxes again are ideas that may be helpful to you. The purpose of this chapter is to get you thinking about the different types of taxes and how they may apply to you. If you get in front of a professional, a good trustworthy professional in your area that not only understands investments but also taxes, they can help structure the proper plan for you. We would advise you to seek out an investment advisor that completely understands taxes and tax saving strategies. Not a tax person that thinks they understand investments, because those are very few and far between. If you talk to an investment advisor that really understands taxes they can improve your cash flow and do some very, very interesting things so that you don't pay more taxes than you have to, and the idea is you have more spendable income. The goal is more after-tax income for those critical retirement years. have more spendable income. The goal is more after-tax income for those critical retirement years.

Annuities - Annuities can be set up to provide a very, very favorable tax treatment which should increase your spendable income meaning your after-tax income. It's important to think about and plan for the early years of your retirement when you are able to do many things. We call this the go-go stage. Then plan for the later years of life when maybe you don't have the energy or the physical ability to do the things you used to be able to do. We call those stages the slow-go stage, and the no-go stage. It's about maximizing your spendable income when you need it the most and then maybe you pay a little bit more in taxes in the later years of your life when you may not be as physically active to spend the extra money anyway. It's just some smart tax planning here.

TAX PREPARER VS. TAX PLANNER

As we close this chapter, once again, let us emphasize the importance of taxes and tax planning on your overall finances and income. The new Tax Reform Bill and changes therein should and could have dramatic impact on your overall taxes. Up to this point you may have been only using a 'tax preparer' to do your taxes; going forward there may be great benefit in utilizing a "tax planner". A tax planner doesn't just look back to the last 12 months and tell you what you have to pay in taxes, they look ahead one year, three years, and even five years and beyond, and plan for strategies to pay less in taxes going forward. This is huge to your overall nest egg and retirement. Feel free to call the Beacon Capital Management offices to set up a free consultation with our tax planning professional.

CHAPTER 4:
PLAN FOR INFLATION AND LONGEVITY RISK

There are two main reasons why inflation is so critical to plan for. The first reason is that we're living longer, the second reason is because of the fiscal policy of the United States. Because we're borrowing more and more money, there's a high probability that inflation at some point in our lifetime could be worse than what we've experienced in the decades of the '90s and the 2000s. But the main thing we want to focus on here for this particular chapter is the longevity risk.

Statistics tell us that if we're sitting down with a couple that are both age sixty-five, there is a high possibility that one of them (if not both of them) will live into their nineties. If you think back thirty years ago and somebody would die at age sixty-five we would say, "oh they lived a good life". Now if somebody dies at sixty- five we say, oh my goodness they died so young. Just think about how our mentality has changed towards longevity.

Well, add to that the fact that medicine is getting better, doctors are able to keep us alive longer, we're much better educated now about nutrition and fitness and so on. Most of the families we see that are retired are living very, very vital and meaningful lives. They are volunteering in their communities and waking up in the morning with vigor for life. Those people are going to live for a much longer time, so it is key that we factor inflation into their retirement income plan.

> **RETIREMENT CAN LAST 25 TO 30 YEARS; YOU NEED A STRATEGIC PLAN FOR INFLATION!**

I think at a minimum you should count on at least 3% inflation per year. We have families that come in to us and we engage in a conversation with them about this. Some of them are concerned with much higher inflation rates and so we'll factor that into their income plan. But count on at least 3% inflation regardless. In very simple terms what that means is that if it costs you $5,000 a month to live this year, the next year you'd better have $5,150 a month, and the following year you would have to have $5,314.50 a month, and so on. You need to be able to give yourself 3% raises every single year. At current interest rates that is why just taking all your money and putting it in the bank and collecting interest usually is not a good solution for most of us. It's in our best interest to factor in at least 3% inflation.

Historically speaking, if we go back over a thirty-year period, inflation has been at around 3%. If you're concerned about government policies, about U.S. borrowing, the national debt, our constant budget deficits, and all the promises that we've made as far as Medicare and Social Security, then you might want to factor in a 4% or 5% long-term inflation rate to your retirement plan. If you go online and play with some of those income calculators or those retirement calculators that are available on Vanguard and Fidelity and T. Rowe Price and so on and you start factoring in 5% inflation, you'll find out very quickly you'd better be getting very good rates of return on your money to keep up with that inflation. So inflation planning is critical. When we plan for our clients, we plan for a minimum of at least 3% for inflation.

Let's talk about some investments that can help protect you against inflation. We've already mentioned some of these things, but we want to touch on them one more time. So first of all, real estate has historically been a tremendous hedge against inflation. That's primarily because real estate reflects replacement costs of the assets. For example, a seven-story office building may have been built about twenty or twenty-five years ago. To build the exact same building today would cost much more than it did then. This is because the steel, the sheetrock, the concrete, all the electrical, the pipes, all of those materials cost much more today. Therefore, that building built twenty-five years ago is worth much more than it was when it was first built. Why? Because the replacement cost is much higher.

If you owned this building, you've been collecting rent all those years and there have been two things that have happened over time. One is you've been able to raise the rent because again, as inflation kicks in, renters have to pay more money, and if you're a landlord collecting that rent, your income goes up along with inflation. Secondly, the value of the building that you own goes up because the replacement cost is more. So you are not only getting raises on your cash flow, but you're also able to sell the building at a future date for much more than you paid for it.

Now this doesn't always work in the short-term. Some of you are thinking right now about what happened in the real estate collapse in the U.S. and commercial real estate market in the U.S. in 2008. We understand that, but that is a relatively short-term period and has not been typical. If you're planning for retirement, you're planning on ten, twenty, thirty years or more of retirement; then we think real estate can be one good inflation hedge to consider.

Another good inflation hedge to own could be stocks. The problem with stocks is that we have to watch them go up and down every single day. But stocks as an asset class, what you really have there is ownership in companies. If you're not trying to beat the market and just buy real hot stocks and you are buying really good companies that you think are going to be around for a long time, then you should certainly keep up with inflation as far as value goes. Let's just think about a few here together, Coca Cola, General Electric, United

Technologies, AT&T, Wal-Mart, Kimberly Clark, and Merck, which is the big pharmaceutical company. Those types of companies, good healthy companies that have a lot of cash flow, should be around for a long time. The values of those businesses should go up over time, or at least if you have a basket of 100 stocks, most of the business values will go up over time. In addition, as mentioned earlier, you can collect some dividends. So stocks can be a very good inflation hedge. Now again, the problem with stocks is people don't want to see them go up and down. You get a statement in the mail and when your account is down 10-20% from just three months earlier that's very unsettling, and you begin to wonder if you'll ever recover. So stocks are not appropriate for everybody, and they certainly may not be appropriate for too much of your portfolio in retirement. But we're mentioning them here as an inflation hedge.

So we talked about real estate and we've talked about stocks. Now, in addition to that, a pretty good hedge against inflation can be an annuity that will give you increases in income over time. Right now there's a big insurance company that we use fairly often that you can receive increasing income as an inflation hedge on your income. It's kind of like having a COLA (cost of living allowance) on your pension or Social Security income.

When you begin to take income off of this annuity, you'll take the income value of the annuity and if you happen to be sixty-five, they'll start you out at 5% of whatever the value is. So let's say the value is $500,000 and you're sixty-five. They're going to start paying you $25,000 a year. That $25,000 a year is guaranteed for the rest of your life, no matter how the underlying account does. In addition to that, every year that the stock market indexes go up, you will get a raise. So every few years in that annuity you should get a raise that will in a sense give you kind of a cost of living allowance raise like a pension does. This is very attractive and also comforting. So, as you can see, some annuities can be a decent inflation hedge if they're the right kind. Again, not all annuities work like this; they have to be the right kind.

Other assets that may protect against inflation would be direct ownership of things like oil or natural gas. You could have some precious metals or an exchange traded fund or a mutual fund that invests in precious metals. This can become very risky, so you have to be very careful in that area.

One particular investment that you could also use is something called master limited partnerships. This can be a very attractive inflation hedge and it can also pay you a very nice income. For example, there is a company called Kinder Morgan; they own pipelines all across the United States. They're underground pipelines where natural gas and oil are piped through and sometimes they're over ground. What Kinder Morgan does is they basically own the pipe and then if Shell Oil wants to ship oil or natural gas from the port of Houston up into Denver for instance, they run it through Kinder Morgan's pipelines, and Kinder Morgan collects a toll, if you will, on that oil and gas. Think of Kinder Morgan as charging rent to Shell Oil to occupy their pipeline. Well, because you're getting rent off the pipeline, you're getting an income, but also remember the replacement cost of the pipeline, just like real estate, is going up in value. So that can act over time as an inflation hedge. This gives you another option to invest in something that can potentially help protect against inflation.

The last inflation hedge we want to mention is the inflation-protected bonds put out by the U.S. government. You can buy what is called I Bonds from the federal government or you can buy a fund that invests in I Bonds. We don't typically do a lot of these because the results have been fairly disappointing to many investors but then again, others have been pleased. These are likely to perform better if and when inflation begins to increase. These have been especially appealing to those who love the fact they are backed by the U.S. government and deemed therefore to be very safe.

The point of this chapter in particular has been to get some ideas so that you are better prepared for the possibility of having a 20 to 30 year-long retirement. The goal has not been to give individual or specific recommendations to you, as we don't know your overall situation; what our goal has been though is to show there are many options to consider in keeping your purchasing power above that of inflation. If we get a chance to visit with you one on one, then we can explore more specific strategies to fit your goals, risk tolerance and needs.

CHAPTER 5:
SELECTING YOUR FINANCIAL ADVISOR

"Wall Street is the only place that people ride to in a Rolls Royce to get advice from those who take the subway" - Warren Buffett

> **"SELECTING THE RIGHT FINANCIAL ADVISOR FOR YOUR RETIREMENT YEARS COULD BE THE DIFFERENCE BETWEEN SUCCESS AND FAILURE!"**

In his book Confessions of a Happy Christian, author and motivational speaker Zig Ziglar tells the story of flying back to his home in Dallas when he notices the man sitting next to him is wearing his wedding ring on his index finger instead of the third finger on his left hand, which is what most people call the "ring finger." Zig says he couldn't resist the temptation to comment on this anomaly, so he leans over and says, "Friend, I can't help but notice that you have your wedding ring on the wrong finger." The man smiled and replied, "Yeah, that's because I married the wrong woman!"

When undertaking any endeavor, whether it is business, personal or financial, deciding who you will partner with is crucial to the success of the venture. Choosing the right financial advisor can make the difference between having a happy, worry-free retirement or one fraught with concern. Just as finding the right match in most any endeavor you can name is important to its success, the firm you select to assist you with your financial future needs to be a good match. The people you work with must have your interest at heart and share your values. The decision, of course, is a personal one, but there are several criteria that it would be prudent to consider in making it. Here are a few:

ARE THEY INDEPENDENT?

What you don't want to do is select as your financial advisor someone who is an employee of a large firm. Whose interests do you think that individual will be representing – yours or the employer?

Virtually anyone can hang out a shingle advertising himself or herself as a financial advisor. They may offer even be able to offer solutions to your financial problems, but at the end of the trail the solutions will usually result in your buying products that the company is selling. It is not uncommon for such firms to have certain products or offerings that it is in their best interest to sell you. The managers tell their "advisors" what funds to recommend to clients, not because these funds are necessarily what you need to reach your investment goals, but because it benefits the brokerage house. The advisor's job is not necessarily to enhance your financial situation, but to increase the value of the company's stock shares and enhance the pocketbooks of shareholders. There is nothing illegal about this. Like any other enterprise in America, they are in business to make a profit. But if you choose a Wall Street brokerage firm as your advisor, you are unlikely to find individuals who will educate and inform you and then allow you to make independent choices. An independent advisor has no obligation except to you. An independent financial advisor answers, not to a board of directors, but to you and you alone.

ARE YOU DEALING WITH A FIDUCIARY?

Now there's a word you don't use very often in everyday conversation. What does it mean? The word "fiduciary" comes from the Latin word, "fiduciarius," meaning "to hold in trust". The word connotes a legal or ethical relationship of trust between two or more parties. The root word of "fiduciary" is the Latin "fides," which means true. Cousin words that share the same root are "confidential," "fidelity" and "bona fide," all of which have to do with faithfulness and trust.

In the financial world, a fiduciary has pledged to work for the interests of his or her client and swears to put that client's interests ahead of his or her own. The advice fiduciaries give is always client-driven as opposed to profit-driven. The best type of fiduciary is a Registered Investment Advisory Firm (RIA). This simply means that financial professionals within this firm have made an official pledge, at the risk of losing their license and their livelihood to place their client's interests ahead of their own without exception. RIAs are subject to audits by state and/or federal government securities regulators to ensure this is happening.

DO THEY UNDERSTAND YOU?

Have you ever noticed that when you visit the doctor's office for your annual physical exam the nurse hands you a clipboard with several forms to fill out? It may irritate us to have to fill them out again when we gave them the same information last year, but the forms are necessary. Your health situation may have changed in the last 12 months. The doctor will ask you several questions during the face-to-face portion of the exam, too. Why? Because a good physician will want to know everything about you physically before he treats you. A competent doctor would never prescribe medication for you without first having a complete understanding of your physical condition and knowing any other medication you are taking.

A competent financial advisor will be one who takes the time to thoroughly understand your financial situation. He or she will spend time listening to you so as to ascertain not only what your financial goals are, but why. A competent financial advisor will formulate a plan to execute your wishes. You want to work with a financial advisor who has no product to push and no other agenda to follow except yours.

DO THEY THINK LIKE YOU?

By this we don't mean that they must agree with you on personal issues or share your taste in music and entertainment. Of course not! But when it comes to your money it is crucial that they share your values. If you are nearing or in retirement, your resources are precious to you because of what they represent – independence, quality of life. If you are not willing to treat those assets as if they were fodder for the gambling casinos in Las Vegas, then neither should they. And yet we have heard horror stories of where that appears to have been the case – advisors who are insensitive to the age of their clients and where they are along the financial timeline. If you are like most folks in the red zone of retirement you have a path in mind. You need advisors who will accompany you and help you over the obstacles in that path – not ones who will attempt to lead you to a different path just because it is one more familiar to them. Let us give you an example:

In our RIA firm our goal is preserving your wealth and putting assets to work in such a way that your income is supplemented without depleting your principal, where possible.

When potential clients come to our office for a consultation, the first thing we do is chat. We want to know what is on their mind. What are their notions about money and finances? We want to be able to match our thinking with theirs so we can work together. But if we can't, there is no need to proceed. We part as friends, but we are not a match for everyone and we do not try to be.

Sometimes we find it useful to ask potential clients to pretend that all their money was cash and stacked up in their living room. Sounds crazy, but it helps put things in perspective. Here's all this money in your living room. What should you do with it? You can't just leave it there. If you invest it, what should be the primary attribute of this investment? What do you want the money to do for you and your family? We usually find that after this kind of a conversation we and our clients share the same core beliefs about money and the path forward becomes easier to chart. Our priorities are usually in the same order:

- Safety
- Growth/Income/Returns
- Taxes/Fees
- Liquidity

Yes, safety first of all, then growth. Keep in mind that we specialize in handling cases where the individual is approaching or in retirement. Our philosophy at Beacon Capital Management is it's not the money you make but the amount you get to keep that counts. What good is growing your wealth only to let it slip away?

HOW ARE THEY COMPENSATED?

In your search for the right advisor be sure to find out how the advisor candidate is paid. If you are paying them, then they work for you. If a brokerage house, or some other major firm, is paying them, then they don't work for you. It's as simple as that. They work for someone else. Don't be embarrassed to ask, "How are you compensated?" That is not a personal question; it is a business question. It is appropriate fact-finding. You are not asking that to be nosy or to find out the advisor's yearly salary or net worth. You want to know if there are possible conflicts of interest or hidden fees and charges. Knowing how your advisor is compensated may help you understand and evaluate how objective he or she will be in any recommendations you receive. True professionals will not mind this dialogue between client/advisor at all.

HOW WILL THEY WORK WITH YOU?

There should be a high level of communication between you and your financial advisor. Do not hesitate to ask what the firm's policy is on periodic reviews of your portfolio. Also ask who will be handling your account? Will it be farmed out to a third-party firm? Or will the advisor candidate you are interviewing be the one who personally handles the account? If other team members will be involved in managing your account, wouldn't it be a good idea to meet and get to know them?

When you call the number of the office, will a human answer the phone during business hours? Or will you have to listen to a series of impersonal prompts that ask you to enter information repeatedly, only to then be connected to someone's voice mail? We know some people who are computer literate and up-to-date on modern technology. They understand voice mail when the person they are calling is unavailable. But they get frustrated when they have to press one for English and two for Spanish and then digitally enter their date of birth, pin number, account number and zip code, only to have to listen to another menu of choices. We can't say we disagree with them.

WHAT OTHER SERVICES DO THEY OFFER?

Service is important in financial planning. How often will they meet with you to discuss your progress? The financial landscape is constantly changing. Your needs and your thinking may change, too. You need to meet with your advisory firm at least once a year, maybe more often than that, to keep pace with these changes.

Lastly, do you like this person? What is your gut telling you about this person? Don't ignore this. Your gut instinct is mostly right in measuring trust. Feelings, after all, are facts. Do you feel that you can trust this individual to be an advocate for you in this important area of life?

RETAIL VERSUS INSTITUTIONAL INVESTING

There is a tremendous advantage when ordinary folks have the services of institutional-level advisors and consultants. These professionals can often help investors to bypass the additional costs of the retail brokerage market. Institutional account holders generally trade directly without the extra costs associated with retail distribution and marketing. Call it cutting out the middle man if you wish, and, in the bargain, getting someone who will tell you the truth, the whole truth, and nothing but the truth about your financial affairs. Individual investors who receive institutional-level advice benefit from having professional managers and financial planners focusing on their overall allocation and the active movement of capital to attractive areas from unattractive ones. It's the difference between active management and the staid "buy-and-hold" philosophy of investing that is no longer an effective way to navigate the risks presented by today's geographically diverse, fast- paced financial markets. This is especially true for retirees. Of all investor classes, these folks are making critical allocation decisions with the portion of their portfolios they place in the stock market. They deserve full-time, institutional-level professionals working on their behalf and to be directly accountable when making the really important investment allocation decisions.

IT'S WORTH THE EFFORT

Selecting the right retirement advisor will require some work on your part, but it's worth it when you consider just how critical your decisions about money are when you approach retirement. Getting it right is the difference between losing sleep and having peace of mind. Selecting the right guide for this part of your financial journey can mean being able to enjoy your golden years instead of worrying about them. Let's face it – retirement is unfamiliar territory. There is the possibility for great adventure but also potential danger if you fail to prepare properly. To make sure you take the right steps, you want as a guide an individual who knows the landscape and can get you through it safely with money enough for the rest of your life.

AUTHOR NOTES

In conclusion, the book you have in your hand presents some basic concepts for succeeding with money for the new year. This book is not meant to be the be-all and end-all, and discuss every single detail of different investments you can have, and certainly is not a writing on economic policy. It's just a means to keep things simple and hopefully shift your thinking as a retiree or as somebody who is planning towards retirement so that you can have more confidence in what you're doing and to give you some direction whether you use a financial advisor or not. When you find that retirement coach, that financial advisor who is the right person and you feel understands and cares about you, and has your best interest at heart; when you find that right person, you will be able to enjoy a wonderful and happy retirement.

Investment Advisory Services offered through Beacon Capital Management, LLC, an SEC Registered Investment Advisor.

Made in the USA
Columbia, SC
21 December 2020